This is my book

My Name is:

_____

MOMMY AND DADDY ARE GETTING A DIVORCE

by

Erin Lynn

Book Design and Production by Contact Lynns Publishing
Front Cover Design by Tori Lynn
Editing by Ronyea Thompson

Contact Lynn's Publishing
TheLynnses.com
214-997-4077

Thank you

My Heavenly Daddy, thank you for Saving us and Loving us and Teaching us and taking care of us. You Are Awesome.

To my Grandmama K and Granddaddy J and my aunties K and A, thank you for always loving us and our mommy. I love you so much.

Great grandpa Lt Ponds and grandma Mae H. Ponds (RIH), Thank you for loving on us and trying to teach big people, "Kids are people too, they're just in little bodies."

Thank you to Kim Wesson (Autumn, Jalen), Mr. Cris McFadden, Acting Coach Mr. Larome Armstrong, Cousins Charles and Taiwannika Walker (Tai'Charle, Braeden, Cameron), Mr. Isaac Lee, Ms. LaFonda (Michelle, Maria), Mr. Andy Brown, Ms. Michelle Davis (Parker, Hunter), Mr. Kelvin Edwards, Mrs. Skipper, Mrs. Summer, and Imogene (RIH) for the great things you've done for us.

Thank you to Auntie Ronyea, Uncle Ray, Auntie NiChelle, Uncle Michael, Uncle Scottie, Uncle Rob, cousins The Bryants, Willie, RaiDion, Ryleigh, and Robbie for loving us.

To my grandma "GG" Author Jerri Lynn, for spoiling us and teaching us how to be BIG little kids.

To my mommy, Author Tori Lynn, I LOVE YOU MOMMY!!!

Table of Contents

Mommy and Daddy
are getting a divorce

"Mommy and Daddy are getting a divorce," my parents said. That's all! But, they didn't help me understand. All I know is, a divorce doesn't sound like something good.

So, what is a divorce? Why do they want to get one? They said they loved each other. So does this mean they don't love each other anymore? What's going to happen to me? Where am I going to live? Are they getting a divorce because of me? If they get mad at me are they going to divorce me? Will they stop loving me too? Why can't they work it out? What is a Divorce?

What is a divorce?

Dear Divorce,

I'm writing you because you are what parents use to help break up families. What do parents use to help families stay together? Since everyone else is writing you for help, I guess I will write you for help too.

At school we learn arithmetic: add, subtract, multiply and divide. I have learned that you are a divider. You give families a way to pull apart, live apart, and think apart. Life with you is causing everything to fall apart. They need to call you division from now on because that's what you are doing. My family is divided now. Everyone is fighting about you: mom and dad, brothers and sisters, my brother and my mom, grandma and dad,

mom and dad's friend. Everyone is

DIVIDED!

I'm a kid!

Dear Divorce,

Derek's mom and dad are divorced. Sometimes she will say mean things about Derek's dad or call him names. But she always say how much Derek looks and acts like him. Derek feels that she's mad at him for looking like his dad. It makes him sad. Derek told his grandma, "Just because I look like daddy doesn't mean that I am him. I love my mom but I also love dad. I don't try to look like him and I don't try to act like him. I don't know how I am supposed to act. I only know what I've learned."

Divorce, please ask my mom not to talk about my dad because that would make me feel bad. Please let my parents remember that I'm the kid.

Don't forget about me

Dear Divorce,

Jeff's parents' are divorced. Jeff's dad often forget to come pick him up for the weekend. When Jeff's dad doesn't come, Jeff gets sad. Sometimes Jeff's mom calls Jeff's dad and yell at him.

Divorce, please ask my dad to remember to come and get me when all of this is over.

In the Middle

Dear Divorce,

What is child support? My friend, Maria's, mom and dad are divorced but her mom won't let her go with her dad on the weekends, because he won't give her mom money to help take care of Maria and her brother. This makes Maria sad because sometimes she wants to go with her dad. Sometimes she wants to go skating but dad won't help.

She said, one night she heard her mom talk about the child support order. This will make Maria's dad help her mom with money and make her mom let them go with their dad some weekends. They all loved each other before so why do the child support order to help them to remember the kids.

Divorce, remind my mom and dad to not use us to hurt each other. Also, remind them to think about us before they are ordered to.

What do I do with my feelings?

Dear Divorce,

Some say that my brother Cadence

is getting bad or they don't know what's

gotten into him. Well I don't think he

knows either. What are we are supposed

to do now that our parents don't want

each other anymore?

So, what do we do now? Cadence is not trying to be bad or act different no one is helping him understand his feelings. Maybe if he understood them, then he would behave differently.

Divorce, please give my parents other ways to help us show our feelings. Maybe we can talk to the school counselor, big brothers and sisters, or a place we can talk to people who can help us understand what's happening and help us understand our feelings.

Also, help them remember that they are not the only ones going through the divorce because the kids are going through the divorce too.

We're just kids

Dear Divorce,

Elsa's dad, Mr. Knight, hits Elsa a lot. He tells her mom that Elsa and her baby sister are bad. Grandma Knight said they act like wild animals. Elsa begs her mom not to send her back to her dad's but when her mom tries not to send her back, Elsa's dad calls the police on Elsa's mom.

Elsa's dad hit her two-year-old little sister Kacey for having an accident and hit her one-year-old teething baby brother for biting Elsa.

Divorce, when this is over, please ask my parents to remember we're kids and not hit us all the time. The divorce is hard enough.

What about us?

Dear Divorce,

Rick lives with his dad. Ricks' mom sometimes will pick Rick up and drop him over his grandma's house leaving him there for hours or sometimes the whole weekend. It makes him sad when they don't spend much time together.

Divorce ask my parent not to come

get me if they are going to drop me off

somewhere else. I'd rather stay home and

play with my toys. Please don't act like

you don't want to be bothered or drop

me off over someone else's house. Let's

keep our special time.

I'm okay

Dear Divorce,

I'm brave, I'm smart, and I'm important. I'm going to be strong for my siblings and for myself. I will try not to add any stress to my parents. I will clean my room and do chores like put away the dishes or take out the trash. I will try and

make good grades. Usually parents are excited about that. And when I'm feeling sad I will write, draw, or say what I feel. I will use my words. My feelings matter. The divorce is not my fault.

All we need is

LOVE!

Also Look for:

By Tori Lynn

The Divorce

The Battle

By Erin Lynn

Mommy and Daddy are getting a divorce

By Ryan Lynn

My Feelings Matter

TheLynnses.com